DOUBLE

John Hartley Williams was born in Cheshire and grew up in North London. He was educated at William Ellis School, and at the universities of Nottingham and London. He now teaches English at the Free University of Berlin, where he has been since 1976. He has also lived and worked in France, Francophone Africa, Yugoslavia, and 'one spent an abominable year in Bristol, England'.

His first book, *Hidden Identities*, was published by Chatto in 1982. He won the £5000 first prize in the Arvon International Poetry Competition in 1983 with 'Ephraim Destiny's Perfectly Utter Darkness', the centrepiece of his maverick second collection *Bright River Yonder*, a baroque Wild West poetry adventure published by Bloodaxe Books in 1987 (and a Poetry Book Society Recommendation). Bloodaxe have also published his later collections *Cornerless People* (1990) and *Double* (1994).

He has organised poetry readings by visiting poets in Berlin, has promoted poetry workshops there, and was chief perpetrator of two Bloodaxe poetry festivals in Berlin in 1989 and 1992.

DOUBLE

JOHN HARTLEY
WILLIAMS

BLOODAXE BOOKS

ISBN: 1 85224 273 6

First published 1994 by
Bloodaxe Books Ltd,
P.O. Box 1SN,
Newcastle upon Tyne NE99 1SN.

Bloodaxe Books Ltd acknowledges
the financial assistance of Northern Arts.

Cover printing by J. Thomson Colour Printers Ltd, Glasgow.

Printed in Great Britain by
Bell & Bain Limited, Glasgow, Scotland.

i.m. David Williams
1909-1983

Acknowledgements

Acknowledgements are due to the editors of the following publications in which some of these poems first appeared: *Der 8 Dortmunder Lyriknacht vom Verein fur Literature e.v.*, *Foolscap*, *Hard Times* (Berlin), *Klaonica: poems for Bosnia* (Bloodaxe Books/ *The Independent*, 1993), *The New Poetry* (Bloodaxe Books, 1993), *The Poetry Book Society Anthology 3* (PBS/Hutchinson, 1992), *Poetry Review*, *Poetry with an Edge* (Bloodaxe Books, new edition, 1993), *The Rialto* and *The Wide Skirt*. Some have been published in performance at Morden Tower (Newcastle), Bernard Stone's Turret Bookshop (London), Marga Schoeller's Bookshop (Berlin), The British Bookshop (Checkpoint Charlie, Berlin), Der 8 Dortmunder Lyriknacht (Dortmund), Literaturstadt London, Literarisches Colloqium (British Council, Wannsee) and Poetry with an Edge, Theatre 89 (Neue Gesellschaft fur Literatur, Berlin).

Contents

The marvellous thing about a joke with a double meaning is that it can only mean one thing.

RONNIE BARKER

Looking Over The Wall

There used to be platforms.
Their purpose was for seeing over,
& I climbed the steps at dusk, & saw over.
There was a solitary rabbit, & a man with a shoot to kill policy,
& far off, a jeep without lights.
Next to me a man was explaining to his wife
in a language that cd have been anything,
well...what *was* he explaining...?

He was telling his wife of the golden city,
of the plump city fathers, the kindly & democratic trade,
of the young men who came hungrily looking,
whose honesty wd not permit them to steal,
whose incorruptibility won them the merchant's daughter,
& of the laughing infants in the Gardens of the Wheel.
Then they stopped & looked at me,
& they smiled & sd something that might have been:
'You are blessed.'

And I nodded & stood alone, looking over,
at a man with binoculars, looking back.

Riding the Wall

We pedalled along its circumference
On a sunny day, reading

Every grey, admonitory inch.
Our spokes blurred as we chatted.

On the other side there were messages, too,
And an army of people tearing them up.

You cd peep thru cracks & watch them:
Soldiers sowing confetti from a shredder bag,

Historical progress of the elderly, following them like crows,
Bending with trembling knees to retrieve what had fallen.

Then there was the place where we stopped
And laid down the bikes,

Stretched out flat on our backs,
And stared at the sky.

Ausländer

The S-bahn rumbled thru dead stations to Friedrichstrasse,
Hanging station boards in Gothic script...

Just a few lights, & a soldier watching us pass,
The exit stairs walled up, & my eyes meeting no one's gaze.

Ears of paper in the crestfallen hands of Turks.
A couple of tourists, looking shrewdly at each other's knees.

The policemen sat deep in lit cubicles. Their eyes wore no faces.
On the command, I met those eyes full on.

Emerging, I saw the sun make the sign of a cross,
High up, on the glass orb of the TV tower.

Or was it just my imagination?
At any rate, I said the word 'foreigners!' angrily.

If it was a curse, well...
It was only a charm against goblins with pitchforks,

Like myself.

Panorama

'Look at that white ribbon!
There it is!'

Something to be observed from the air
as the plane flew west...

No longer. Everyone
rushed across

when they pulled it down,
& I remained behind, contemplating

The Wall, The Secret Garden, The Bitter Dispute,
The Scar, The Object of Desire, Our Constancy.

'It's almost
beautiful from up here, isn't it?'

And my complicity with this speech,
like the shadow of a plane skimming too quickly over ground,

passing over a Wall, that has never been an obstruction to it,
as a dreamer does, sometimes, without understanding

that powerful vindication
of the need to fly.

The City

Nothing in this place is true
The guest rooms are full of dictators
And the girls at the bus stop are rheumatic
They breathe an aroma of garlic & leaves

The city belongs to its monks
Who symbolise their disappearance with howls
Vanishing into candour like someone
Showing you their ugliest room

It belongs to the postman & his girl
They feed their letters on sleep
They keep a nocturne in the corner
It is silent when they struggle by the wall

The city belongs to its idealists
They have pots with windmills in, that turn
As I do, in the breath of others
On balconies & corners until the dawn

The city belongs to its daughters
Who are pale & restless & full fleshed
Taking torches down to the vaults
To betray felicity with secretarial fingers

Tonight I spit cherry pips
Deep into the stove of despair
I can hear them carrying their kitchens
Secretly out into the garden. Why?

'Come here,' I tell you. 'Come here!'
Warm & recalcitrant conundrum that you are
I want to hear you say 'no!' again, hear the mangle
Creaking on the linen that hasn't been washed in years!

Das Doppelgehen

I

In that life the cobblestones
shone with rain. The trams

came clicking by
with streaked-up windows

& faces turned outward to display
what they wd not dream of thinking.

In the leaky hotel
I sat mixing ink with wine

describing
political exhaustion

so brilliantly
you fell in love with me at once.

II

They were more like us
than we were.

Nobody moved a muscle in their symphony orchestra
when they played *The Rite of Spring*.

Their crescendoes were quieter
than our silences.

We sat on a bench
under the dripping boughs of a tree,

a movie of amoral events
viewed thru a mud-splashed windscreen.

That was our taxi
cruising the edges of the park,

with the driver's mirror
turned away.

We bounced down unmade streets
to the end of town,

a *dacha* in a leafless orchard
& a man in a jerkin, waiting...

III

'There I am!' you said.
He was leaning on his gate.

When people discover life is perfect –
there they are.

They fall into a blue drowse.
They smile.

How affably he showed us the way,
when we climbed the stairs to bed,

& the wind blew in like a radio,
& it was just warm enough to be cold!

We felt our blood surge in us like a lie,
& our mouths wd have met over & over,

had the door not banged open,
& he not stood there, petrified,

moving his lips
without a sound...

IV

We stopped kissing, laughed
& invited him in

& gave him Schnapps, & he watched
the cool swoop of yr bodice below yr neck

& yr pale skin sinking
under the horizon

down into that shadow life
beyond the lip of tall buildings,

a narrow cleft, falling & floating
towards an imaginary bliss,

where pleasant words
died mutely in yr arms.

Westberlin Thursday

It was one of those particularly lubricious mornings.
Cars failed to start. Panthers were prowling.

On the other side of The Wall they were burying corpses.
Whose corpses we wd have liked to know?

A chain of towers built by vandals stretched
from the green forest to the beginning of city streets

& we cd hear crying occasionally,
as if children had been punished appropriately for playing with knives.

Next to the dogs, which ran hither & thither on wires,
lay the sky, where it had fallen down

& nobody thought to pick it up, nail it back,
but all walked round it, talking so hard,

you wd have thought it was just a natural obstruction.
The crying was overlaid with a radio playing songs.

We were disturbed by this. I won't say upset.
Sitting on the bus I had a vision of acrimony.

It was upon a computOgraphic wall in the city,
a crucified snarl, with a text underneath it, at the junction

of *Joachimsthaler & Kurfurstendamm*, I
did not have time to read before we passed,

& so remained not wiser, but tantalised,
like a reader whisked past a bookshop.

At this point the number 48 bus
turned into a freedom ferry, bound for islands,

& we sat back, undisturbed by the linden boughs
cracking our rooftop, or the shrieks of the driver

beside himself with rage at the traffic.
'Full ahead engines!' we thought to ourselves.

Our oilsoaked engineers were boozing in the hold,
honest Scotsmen shouting *'Liberty or Death!'* above the hammering...

Yet the ship was threatening to break up from the menace
of charm, politeness & ambition on the bridge,

& rumour had it there were lions in the corridors
with bits of trouser & Italian shoe in their teeth.

Strange how the Captain of a ship is never visible
except in the dreams of confused passengers, who long

for a security that is partly compounded of rape.
There were ten people visible who might have been Captains,

and in the toilets the unlockable doors banged open
to reveal them in uniforms & braid, with girlie books on their bare knees.

I was disquieted, but confident I knew at least
where *I* was going. I found my way to the Stateroom

& extinguished the light. My hunger transmuted
to a metal I cd only work in the dark.

I saw Miss Davenport crawling under the tables toward a glass of water
& grasped her wrist at just the moment

light fell thru the crystal, like dissolving aspirin,
& her smile came to the surface, an apparition of teeth.

Whose secretary? I wanted to know. She knew everything.
I knew that I would have to know her knowledge,

the comings & goings, the leavings & grievings,
if the young men in uniforms at night cried in her arms,

if she was active in relief agencies, oppression agencies,
if, as our hands locked around that glass of water,

there was anything else that was as brilliant,
any other drops of brightness I cd grace with a name,

that might fall, as she did, into my mouth,
from a pure spring in the heart of the chandelier,

our own relenting Miss Davenport, giving out information,
the cold & tasteless clarity of that draught,

as I quaffed it down & felt
the shiver of dishonour hold me fast.

On the Island

All around the National Gallery
are Poles selling their inheritance to Turks.

'This samovar cost me 22 marks!'
says one Turk leaving, to another arriving.

It's Tuesday. Even if the rest of the week
doesn't happen, you can walk out to Krumme Lanke,

look at the nudists, take yr clothes off yrself,
if you feel like it, or fall in love again at the Polish market,

& have me tell you the story of Henry Rivers,
(at the Polish market),

who had a yellow balloon, in which he breasted the hill
to find his lover, Elvira Cigarettepaper, waving from the next valley,

and he, unable to land, pulled her up into the basket
& as they went up…down came their underthings.

This you can do in Westberlin as you walk between the objects
which Polish people have set out for sale:

a ceramic rolling pin, a large glass horse…
some matching ceramic handled spoons…

And bearing in mind how long these people have travelled,
over what roads, bearing what documents, speaking to what officials,

the beauty of the city seems to reside in that horse
in which I see reflected the buttons on yr shirt,

& my fingers, too fast for the buttons, & the eyes
of the Polish vendor's daughter, from Katowice or Osnowiec.

I am Henry Rivers. This is my balloon.
You my *geliebte* Elvira, my little *Eck-kneipe*,

my Brücke der Einheit across which spies are exchanged,
you are my summer residence by Friedrich Schinkel,

out of Hohenzollern summers & Prussian flatness, you are
the *treffendes Angebot* I find whenever I take a step, & the Polish
      merchant

heads me off into the corners & squares of a city map,
where haggling wears an unpronounceable name, like love. And I
    want to tell him:

'Beware! I saw a lighted bus reversing into darkness!
And its driver was trembling with fear

as a man who sees the only way out of a hopeless parking situation
is to move in a direction formerly considered impossible!'

The fact is, the parking situation has become acute,
so let me recommend to you the after hours dancing cruise,

northwards over the Wannsee holding yr glass horse in one hand,
my fingers undoing yr blouse with the other, while the trumpets
    stagger about like drunks,

& a Man from the East buries his stubble in yr blue-veined throat,
as if it were truly possible to have a *Wirtschaftswunder* on the dance
    floor.

'Forward in disorder!' cry Elvira & Henry, those famous Berliners,
wastrels of the post-war years, making uneconomic miracles

from the simple plot of vanishing when wanted,
rising into the night beneath the pregnant belly of their airship,

yellow stretch marks creaking in warm summer darkness,
while the jazz band below crashes around & finally falls into the water.

The Polish girl slips her fingers into my zip, & draws me toward
    her car
murmuring: *'Das gläserne Pferd ist unbezahlbar, einfach nicht zu*
    bezahlen...'

At her experienced touch, the Palace of Sophie Charlotte crumbles,
& the Pomeranian crows are turned to crystal in midflight,

that slow, beating, sinister flight of the hooded grey,
which Henry reaches out from the basket & firmly takes hold of,

letting it cool & harden in his hand, feeling the cables groan,
as Elvira (for his sake) tries to be as naked as she can...

In the Event of Breakdown...

My car broke down, & I stood
In a windy street at night. The rain
Was spattering the phone box.

From the stopped hulk of my car
To a lighted cell, I walked.
My collar was up against the wind.

I made no calls, but stood in that cabin
And pretended to speak, forming
Her number again & again in my head.

I was a kite of sense, rising
On gust & squall, high over
The thatched *U-Bahn* at Dahlem Dorf.

Was she testing another friend
In her arms? I soared
Deep into her reluctance to answer.

Yet I had not called. The black city
From which I had flown up like a stone, gleamed
With the attention I gave it.

Had she pulled a comb thru the fall
Of her hair? Lamps of desire
Prickled everywhere below me.

And that lustreless boulder, my car,
Rotted its immobility downward,
Down thru the tarmac & the clay.

It was a joke to do nothing. An absurd feigning.
I left the box & walked to the dark vehicle,
Leaving the illuminated place behind me.

The bright money chinked
In my hand, for the rescue call
it seemed superfluous to dial.

Between two poles, I stood there, thinking.
I was
Stalled within the buried city of the sky.

The Turning Point

I lived under the helicopter patrol,
in an area of foxes & nightingales,
where corpses were dumped, quaintly, at night.
Russian generals watched me back my car out
thru holes cut in each raised copy of *Pravda*,
whilst I tried to explain by waving my arms
why a *Tisch* is not a table, a bed is not a *Bett*,
& even why, in another language,
embraces open doors
on which the name plate, tho absolutely incorrect,
may not be absolutely wrong.

Being under surveillance, I needed
the one friend I cd run to in the city.
When the police had set up their roadblocks,
only the anonymous & loving address wd save me.
The nature of that room in which
we found the secret borders, narrow & excitable,
where language ached within its confines,
was just an unromantic ordinariness.
She brought the documents. The kisses.
She was punctual. She always bothered to turn up.
She trembled with efficiency.

At night, when the searchers were restless,
we'd leave a basket of fruit on those shabby stairs,
that dreary hallway where
the tramps wd urinate if the door was not locked,
& someone had written *Ficken tut gut*,
that the *Hauswart* wouldn't clean off.
Then we'd hear steps going up & down, & someone
cursing, the basket kicked over,
& I'd hold her, listening to apples & pears
cascading in profusion
down German steps.

When thousands gathered on the Berlin Wall,
thru a babble of dark celebration we snuggled down,
poring over microfilm of another freedom,
speculating what pictures these were, who had brought them,
whether illustrations of her nakedness,
crushed between two lines of concrete,
were beautiful, or merely
photographers taking liberties for miles?
And as the shouting rose, we wondered:
Did this mean
travel restrictions had been lifted forever?

I ride those fallen limits, now.
The ground's been scuffed with death
our bus bumps over
toward the *Rote Rathaus*, Alexanderplatz.
They're lifted still, the voices in the East,
winter in my skull, a flurry of approaching cold.
I watch as buildings start to disappear,
the road becoming endless. Like
a radio shut off, the shouting
dies, the bus goes deaf. We just
go forward, thru the stealthy air...

```
YOU ARE LEAVING
     THE
BELIEVABLE SECTOR

SIE VERLASSEN DEN
 GLAUBWÜRDIGEN
    SEKTOR
```

Look, We Have Come Thru!

It was our hearts pushed us over
To the proper side of the street,
Where things that might have been
Come true too late.

The sky was full of ruins.
We hurried past the flags,
The throng of empty pedestals,
Buildings like fog.

The Big Dipper was stopped.
Nobody on it.
The thrill of an accident unlikely.
Its cars stalled at the top.

Against an evening of yellow candy-floss,
It rose like a dinosaur's skeleton, gaunt,
Devastated, & thank God, behind us.
No need to hurry after all.

We counted our pennies.
What did you order in a bar here?
They didn't shout at us to sit down,
To hang the coats over there.

Strutting round the tables
Was the local comedian,
Telling jokes that really made us
Groaaaaan...

The way his loudness stammered
Like a man at the end of his tether:
'Too much back to normal here, my friends!'
Was comforting. Rather.

Funny how droll he looked –
Hands thrown up, legs splayed,
Punchlines dragged out endlessly. Every inch
A star, I'd say.

Magic & Peewee in the Rain

(Title observed aerosolled on
the Berlin Wall, 27 March 1990)

Like two lost conscripts
from the stationed eskimo army,
hunting seal out on an ice floe,
they drifted into the city.

They saw that someone
had broken the Republic into huge blocks,
before tossing it into heaps. Left behind
were a few standing chunks.

They wrote their names on it,
first hers, then his. It was drizzling hard.
The ink began to run.
How do you spell it? she said.

His hand printed on her soaking shirt
the outline of her breast. They were lovers.
I watched them as I'd watched those walls calve,
all my sisters, all my brothers.

They were the revolution.
I was the status quo.
They desired. And desired change,
beneath a standstill sky.

By a drab flight of the wall,
he pushed up her skirt,
greedily thrust himself inside.
Something stirred in her throat.

Suddenly undyslexic,
her moans fluttered & soared.
The rain beat back against a picture
of a door flung wide.

Then, pinned by a gust, they clung
to the endless grey,
& were still. She pulled down her hem –
that universal gesture of degree.

He handed her a tissue.
She wiped herself. Two British kids?
How wd she get home without catching cold?
I wonder if they did.

The Kiss

*(On a photograph of an embrace between Leonid Brezhnev & Erich Honecker.
The former President of the GDR was permitted to board a Varig plane
for Chile on 13 January 1993.)*

In raincoat, at airports, I took others
into my arms, like myself.
You trusted me
not to feel what I felt.

So my hat tilted? I always knew
whose side I was on, knew enough
not to feel sincere, or shiver
if our tongues accurately touched.

Don't do as I do, do as I say. I was
the patron saint of painful duty,
arctic decipherer of what was to be done.
My motto reads: *Unravel Me.*

I'd no desires but yrs.
It was constructive to find flesh, occasionally,
as the cameras checked on my suits –
they helped you into my head.

There are clean squares
on the darkened stain of yr walls,
behind them, an orderly garden of frustration:
Zimmerpflanzen, dusty with fraud...

I have gone. That was my picture.
And so have you. With this flight to sanctuary
I erase what's left.
Voluptuaries cancel what they do.

Lights follow me up the ladder.
Blurred night-time pictures show
nothing, as always, nothing, except
the things you imagine I say:

'No exit visa for the sick.
No residence permit for the well.'
But look into the green eyes & sallow face
of my brother, the impassive official,

whose ripped accents are the stick
you lay across my back
in silence, beating & beating
without moving a muscle, like snow.

The Zoo
(for Ken)

Getting there was tricky,
You had to imagine it first.
You imagined *tram* (which never came),
Said yr destination & ran thru the rain.
(Better still, you imagined chair
And stayed at home.)

When you got there, they were careful.
Were you really who you said you were?
(They didn't let *anyone* in.)
If you were, they murmured:
'Someone infectious might have lain beside you.'
It was probably true.

You wanted to see the giraffe,
It had the longest neck in the world, they said,
From trying to look over things. Alas,
That column downward-arched
                              to fallen leaves.
It foraged on the ground
Where once it browsed on trees.

You entered the aviary.
What rained down on you there
Wasn't rain anymore. The inmates were exercising.
They shuffled like a penguin school
Out to the edge of a diving board
With nowhere for a pool.

In mistake for a nap, one of them died.
To celebrate they had a jubilee.
You didn't think much of nature's cheerfulness,
You observed it with a stiff eye.
Be friendly, you thought.
What was the word here for goodbye?

Trying to find the Way Out,
One room led to another, wrongly.
A hippo was receiving bellywash,
Adjusting the vertical hold on its yawn.
A sign upon the wall read:
Last One To Leave Can Keep The Door.

A curved mirror above the Exit
Reflected yr intentions from afar.
If yr visit had been hypothetical,
Going home was a steal.
It very nearly happened
That yr snapshots came back real.

What the Removal of the Wall Left

It left the house on the wall
It left the decision to have built the house
It left the birches: a thin strip of bafflement in the mist
It left the single distant car moving slowly
It required an adjustment of the horizon to the eye
It left the chimney emitting a thin stream of smoke straight up
          into the cold
It left the hooded Pomeranian crow settling on the aerial with a creak
It left the garden that was so small
It left the garden that began to fill with trees that had been planted
It left an overnight population staring thru the trees
It left the trailing hands of the gardener idly touching everything
          in the garden over & over again
It left a worry about the location of asylum
It left a worry about being out on the street
It left foxes running for cover under cars
It left the absence of the nightingales
It left hundreds of removed pictures of legislators
It left a thousand years shrivelled to a day again
It left the unspeakably late arrival of summer
And a tight concentration of pollen in the air

3.X.90 German Reunification Day

'Accessories for disabled drivers,' she says,
'It's in Wembley, Alperton Lane.'
She opens her thirty year old *A Z of London*:
'We go along to Hangar Lane & take the third exit.'
I study the book, in which
Two country roads appear to cross at Hangar Lane.
'I think they've built a few new motorways since then,' I say.
'In fact, there's a roundabout here.'
She takes out her Sherlock Holmes magnifying glass,
And studies the intersection, gravely.
'It's not thirty years old. We kept
Losing copies, don't you remember & having to replace them?
So it's quite up to date really.'

Thru a rainstorm we drive to Hangar Lane
And join the traffic jam. There are flyovers, underpasses,
Howling, high speed carriageways.
And then there is Alperton Lane.
When we arrive a man beckons our car under a roof.
'Come in out of the wet,' he says, & then
Affixes a very large knob to the steering wheel.
My mother looks at it doubtfully.
'How will this make it easier to drive?' she asks.
'Well, you can get a better purchase with it,' says the man, kindly.
I say: 'The problem is, she can only use one hand.'
'We have customers with *no* hands,' says the kindly man.
He has a kind smile. Kindliness itself.
'They steer with their feet.'

After a while, my mother shakes her head.
We drive back over Hangar Lane.
Silent cows are standing in the fields,
Their breath clouding the air. They remind me of
Accessories for disabled drivers, keeping
Their brown eyes thoughtfully on nothing.

Domestic Duties

The old lady wishes
to dispose of rock hard cement.
It will be loaded into the barrow,
driven to the dump.

Squeaking wheels
over the earth, past daffodils. And she
complains, so pretty are they,
their dying takes too long.

Drive to the place
where a concrete slipway falls
to a steel hulk,
empty & smashed & solid.

Let it fall from the platform,
the block that causes strain.
Let it fall from nothing,
to become heavy.

We drive up again thru magnolia,
forsythia branches
whipping the car. Back
thru dull, suburban streets.

Another load. Up to
the departing light of
lawn's edge, where
garden heaps of quiet lie.

Has to be done, what has to.
A silver train beyond the fence
rackets & fades. What used to be so slow
seems endless now, & quick.

Look

At first I didn't see
the thin line he was attached to,
only the man
bent forward on the bench

& staring up...
Then the breeze carried my gaze high
over the building crouched in for years,
over the running track at Gospel Oak,

over poisonous blue –
the vacated swimming pool,
Parliament Hill Café,
open for tough apple pie...

My old school
was a brickfaced kite in heaven,
like an exclamation: *'You there!'*
It stopped me dead.

I watched his wrists
playing the reel. He'd hooked
the past,
made it visible,

& let it rip.
Braced
to that vehement air-shell,
he wrote in swoops

of wind,
his body planted firm
against the tug
of wilful ampersands...

A Wellspent Evening

I

Nice old-fashioned pub: The Westminster,
glass of John Smith's Yorkshire bitter

Get myself reborn
out of the *Evening Standard*

Read about it,
whole day gone up in smoke,
the mugger who pointed a banana at my eyes
& stole a picture of someone I once knew

'Sorry, we don't serve crisps.
Peanuts do?'

I settle down with my pint
& leave the pub

I'm off to see
the expressionist film...

II

Actress alone in bed
sliding her hand
beneath her nightdress

And I think: *'Smoke!'*
smelling the tobacco in my vest
I can feel the sinews of my braces
(I don't wear braces)

I can feel myself clearing my throat,
the slap of my phlegm hitting the quay

Then my clothes get up & dance
for the customers

My stiff black waistcoat
that smells of Africa

My stovepipe trousers etc.
& as I look on at myself

(I hang like a dead coat
on the back of my chair)

I see yr face coming into focus
...ly naked face...

My steel-cleated boots
do a hornpipe on the boards

How can I tell you, I think,
when they take me by the scruff of the neck & throw me out of here,
how can I tell you where to find me
if I don't know where I am?

Can You Hear Me Up There?

There is something I try to remember
that I want to tell you, & always
fail. On the lino my bare feet were cold,
& the light switch, so often
coated with paint, that, brutally,
you snapped off as I read late at night,
made little electrocutive flashes
as it flicked. In the red tiles of
the kitchen, I read till I was blind
all the books, from sink to window &
back. There was a cat outside, on the sill.
I held a poker under the bedclothes,
smart as a soldier, new as a bride.

There were twistings & scuffles, the smell
of privet hedges, & the deprived
privacy of boys. There was the hard feel
of dusty ground in my face. Desire.
I wanted to pick up a weapon & shoot.
There was a carnival also. Pictures of something
I cannot now remember, crudely under
scored as if they might, thru
ignorant radiance, somehow reach words.
You didn't care much about awfulness.
That's what you saw, & said nothing to.
So now I too am silent, in the presence
of others, the presence of betters & wisers.
And what's the point of telling you this anyway?

There's no doubt that all that waiting
in sensual darkness, the dim absurd,
was really the real, the knight with his
rusty armour, creaking upright, a smile
of various kinds on his Welsh face.
You used to get lost in yr armchair notebooks...
Meanwhile you were angry.
There was that recalcitrance of mine.
What image cd you have had of yrself,
considering my own dumb obstinacy of flesh?

I see you at the end, riding the bus
into town, with a review in yr pocket
& a ham sandwich in the other, & I think
if I had an instinct for poverty, straightaway
I'd leave for a distant village, taking
my triple sprung cricket bat, &
some of those black & white photographs
by Harrison Marks, of women, nude,
whiter than yr face when you
caught me smoking, & a few loud records.

And what wd I do there? Well...
It wd be laughable, certainly.
Especially if it rained. And especially
if they jeered at my short trousers,
& the no money I expected kept pouring in,
& my attempts at passing exams proved
(as usual)
to have recaptured the glory of
some fundamental error...

I watch you shrug, & push off
along the seafront with three small boys
in tow. In the middle of yr anger, sometimes,
it stops raining & the day waits.
To me the stillness of weather reflects
always the possibility that something might happen.
If not me, at least one of my brothers
wd certainly do something ridiculous.
The comedy of our empty pockets wd affect you,
& the way you occasionally turned verbal,
you might suddenly decide to board a passing bus,
& we'd skim along the promenade, laughing.
But if that happened (& I don't know if it did),
it's still the way I feel about language:
A complete change of scenery & tempo,
the fleeting fear I might have to start again.

Jack the Lad

Delivering meat on a butcher's bike
With a square steel holder on the front
For a hamper, I kept my mouth open
To catch the groans that dripped from undersides of bridges.

Corpses in my basket, a sawn-off leg,
A pile of lungs like outdoor Japanese inflatables,
I left a trail of blood behind me,
Cheerfully whistling at the stopped-up drains of ears.

Ladies! I said, Ladies! These are
The dissected cadavers of once-were intellectuals!
Chew on this bright & well-informed gristle,
Feel how moist the education of desire becomes!

Behind me the world was pushing
Its puncture & cursing.
I heard my father drive off to work
With a flat cap & a complicated oath.

I was the the undertaker's assistant, the newsboy.
I was the Sonny Jim, the curly knob, the *you-there!* of my generation.
If anyone was introduced to me, they went out & bought pliers & wire;
They stared with slow-directed longing at my toenails.

A man in the park gave me darkness as deep as a well,
'Keep it under yr pillow,' he said, & went off looking strange.
My mother sliced proverbs out of apple peel,
Left me the white quarters on a plate, their bruising flesh.

I didn't tell anyone about the choicest cuts I had.
I wouldn't let the children see them, it wasn't right.
I used to lick them like lollipops in my imagination.
I put the thighs in the attic for later.

But in the end I had to speak out.
They made me stand up at the party and recite female emancipation
Until I blushed. They said I wouldn't have to look intelligent,
But I did of course, & all the delicious frailty turned to jeers.

I'm still the same old sunshine really, tho,
Pedalling round the suburbs like an axeman,
With an ankle sticking out of my pocket, fingers in my hat,
And a couple of ears for buttons.

I've spring-cleaned nightmares to get this far,
And what's wrong with making yr own stuffing,
Especially if you put Christmas in it, some cognac & some poetry,
And talk in a gentle tone to the geese until they put their necks in
     yr hand?

Alice at the Palace

I wandered in the garden
Came to the fountain of phalluses
Twisted, I became straight
Straitened, I became twisted

I did not care for the male member
Except with eyes tightly closed
I suffered its metaphysical intromission
Into my mouth, my behind, my sex

I came to the house
The naked statues were all engaged with one another
Just one or two had time to wink at me
From over a shoulder, or between heavy thighs

I felt the ground rumble
Like the passage of an underground train
I saw the great alley of lime trees
With its Pool of Grace at the end

Out of the brackish water
Came the heads of grinning architects, sprinkling
A fine rain of mist
Camouflaging the fine horses & the Amazon

Who rose greenishly in the centre
Like some kind of denial of my ordinariness
My nice summer dress with the plums on
That Granny made when she was twenty

Water was gulching round their limbs
Woman & horses were in a fine frenzy of the act
I kept trying not to think about
In case I shd get my dress wet

So I bought a ticket for the museum
And went round the dismal rooms
And felt happy there was no fire burning
In the great hall at the centre of the maze

Science Fiction in Hendon Central

I'm walking round what was once a circle of daffodils.
It's straight up-the-hill, all-limousine-action now,
Sky full of boxy clouds, sinister lamp-post invaders.
I pass the girl at the bus stop, smoking...
No *one two three* idling by the tube station,
No top deck passengers reading the cinema placards...

Timetables ripped today. Destinations graffitied out.
Shop windows in rain, the smell of the suburb.
Children giggling near the kissed bosoms of The Quiet Garden.
W.H.Smith's, where I once thought of stealing
Tales of Mystery by H.G.Wells, & read
The Coral Island, a chapter an afternoon.

The Day The Earth Stood Still
I learned the meaning of vivisection, & stared
Terrified at terriers, woeful in amputation. Gave a donation,
And used the rest to enter the ninepennies,
Waited for the spacewoman
To test the warm snout of her lamp on my legs.

Slumped in my seat, too length-stupid to matter,
I watched the steel-boxed robot, more human than human,
Bear lifeless Michael Rennie thru the earthling city.
Her torch moved down the aisle. I imagined her limbs
In the resuscitation cradle, her sweet mouth saying:
'Restore me, Gort! Bring me back to life!'

But when I return from rounding the round,
The girl is no longer there at the bus stop,
Only an old man exercising his dog-having-escaped-amputation.
So I stand & ponder the eternal disappearance:
A mind-circle where flying saucers have landed.
A resolute clockwork fellow. The half-calm streets.

The Multi-Level Underground Car Park is
a Time Machine
(a chronology for motorists)

It rose & fell like a shark,
        the heavy-fender'd coupé,
out of the blue waves of traffic fume,
steeply down the ramp
        to an unlit region.
It dipp't & glid to rest in a stall.

And the lift climb'd,
bearing the chiffon-clad, long-legged beauty
out of the halls of motor Dis
to where the corn lamps of gentle Demeter shine,
in the hotel lobbies, the reception rooms
of nice apartments,
& clerks wear the smiles of reapers...

0000: The Sparking Plug, two poles across which darkness jumps.
1492: Automatic Transmission, smooth as a blind man's hand.

I drive with my eye
on the past.
I burn rubber at multi-colour'd lights.
On six lane highways I occupy all six,
that Cerberus may not pass.

One day, they tell me,
I will have to park my car.

The throb of the motor will die in the lapse't-Catholic darkness,
& the dancing woolly dogs come to rest.
They will shift on back seats, the white limbs of Eros & Psyche,
staining the button'd carriage-cloth with sad, final excitement.
My footsteps will move to the exit,
following arrows
to unspeakable daylight, up the grit of the stairwell.

1653: The Sliding Roof, cold as new minted stars.
1789: The Any Colour So Long As It's Black Revolution.

42

Filthy drays of the rich
creak upon their bloodied tyres;
the salient gloom of the building invades
yr propositions of classic liberal sentiment.

1846: Repeai Of The Horn ட
1945: The Traffic Jam, prodigal drowner of wasps.

Beneath rust thy body is unresting,
stirring & shifting in the shirt of my mind.
Drive you is all that I can, that I will.
Turning in at forbidden intersections,
I chauffeur the forgotten,
entering the past, where the dead
stand alone in the cool, leafbound hush of the trees.

Off the map, off the road, running my handkerchief over the chrome,
seeing their reflection, I hear
whispering branches.
That sweet reciprocation...

City of Gold

Dark-toned bells in the stomach of the candles
Are lit when the Chief Usurer is fleetingly seen

Children carry yellow anxiety in lanterns
Drenched in the fire of their own scribble

The ravens trapped near the station
Croak goodlooking warnings

And the streets are seamed with honey. Only the cab driver
Knows the way to the smoky room

Where ancient hags on the Desire Committee
Urinate ferociously into the cupped hands of skullmakers

Guests in the stilled fountain, gather for a party
Where the neighbour's cool tongue never rests

Where the courtesies hang in the rafters like hams
Where the fish are forever in mid jump

*

Anarchist shop girls throw armfuls of subversion onto the shelves
Readers seize & hold them in trembling hands

Greendog armrests on park benches snarl affection
Strollers settle into their cast iron embraces

Nothing stirs
Except sweet & intelligent breath

Countless sparrows on the scrollwork of buildings form proverbs
Legible only to those who have no faith

And the darkness of truth is an arm holding you close
A troubled music from the throat of a silent sex

*

The sulphur headed girl
Has rawness, the eczema of sainthood between her fingers

The city is a door
Left open on Sunday

Thru which she comes, walking
Like a blaze unravelling paper

And the man who controls the lamps
By making the night rise or fall

Sees light unfasten the skin of trees
He blinks, crouches, hisses, then spits

His tongue slops like water
In the element he has always suspected & feared

He knows she wishes to lift the slab that covers the unknown soldier
She wants to extinguish the eternal flame

Not to pretend that it burns forever
When clearly it is relit for convenience

He knows she wants to erase the inscription
Put something beautiful there, she doesn't know what

He knows she senses the golden thread of words
Leading straight to the heart of magnetism

Where brilliance & fate, a drowse of shadows
Change everything that leaves themselves untouched

                    *

In a low quarter of town
Women tempt you to the pursuit, delicately

They throw kerosene over the nakedness you had not known existed
And set light to it

The line of knowledge tightens
In the fold of the clenching of yr palm

Look for the one who is absent
The constancy she shows is yours

It's the steadiness she walks with that burns you
She won't wait for you to say *Wait!*

Gaze at stars between buildings
Slow the chatter of yr heart

You hold the city in yr hand
Grasped but unsayable

Let silence clarify
The dazzle of the pissed-on years

                    *

The Proving Ground

This is the alphabet
You can make words out of it
Words like *afraid* or *dark*
Phrases like *Have you finished? & Can I go now?*
I'm eating this alphabet. It's made of noodles
Words like *soothe* & *cunt*
I push them around with my knife & fork
And something emerges from beneath the sauce

I often wonder if spelling really exists
The ordinary kind, I mean, that wins prizes
And knows about *i* before *e* except after vanishing
And whether correct spelling tastes better
And if this golden blaze in my head I feel
When I eat the word *touchstone* is really haute cuisine?

Identity Card
(a substitution portrait)

He was at least thirteen parsnips in height
His hair a delicate flamingo pink
He resembled Robin Hood's leaner & meaner brother
He wore an expression of total eclipse
His nose was a distillation of hops & sea air
He had a voice like *Une Saison en Enfer*
And was frequently heard to put the question: Is it love in the rectum?

Subsequently taking up residence in a graveyard
He founded a religion that consisted of asking questions
Such as: Is it love in this graveyard?
Naturally he was fingerprinted by the police
Who used a convenient tombstone as a blotter
And were surprised to read, when the ink had dried:

Empty this

Sad Cases

Language of rain, of smoke blurring the damp haze
Where the wrecked autos, one on one, mimic the grin
Of ultimate standstill. Language of trees, of branches
Grooming the corrugated rooves of sheds, of greenness
Drawn to substance, to the physics of houses...
Language of open doors, of darkness on the sill

Language of lovers, dying thru the morning
Where the beds rattle beyond recall, & the toothbrushes
Crumble in the filthy cup. Language of stench
Of lewd romances, of cookery, of bodies struggling
To exhaust the ways there are to fry an egg
Of making makeshift shift, of tarnishing the city
Corroding it with endless, saturating kisses
Language of dark sentence from the rust of mouths

The Time

Season of yellow sputum, missed cabs & recklessness
Of rain & reversed decisions, of Autumn maybe's
Season of money, of used pound notes, of dollars
Of damp exchange bureaux & sullen Asian ladies
Season of the windswept Bourse & men in hats
Of blowy river walks to the seat of reason
Season of sinking ships & voices thru a neighbour wall
A spattered pane, a tubercular gust, a slammed door...

Season of phone calls, of moralists with no heart
Of thieves hurling stolen goods into the Ark
Season of negatives, of yr careless hands
Of a body turning on the knife of a caress
Season of dreams, of things that didn't happen, did
The hard-edged lineaments of maladresse

John Bosnia

We have the biggest mushrooms in the world.
If you are lucky enough to collect a basketful,
Take them home & cook them.
Wait a year or so. If you're still alive
Buy some more & try again. Either way
The process is definitive.
Then we have Hercegovina, which means (roughly),
The Prince Who Drank (And Keeps Drinking) (And Is
                      In A Perpetual State Of Drinking)
The Wine. We call this the continual case
Which does not exist in yr language. Yet.
Climb our many mountains, you will see a shepherd descending.
For *dvije banke* he will sell you the body
Of his goat. We are hard people. We take our pleasure fiercely.
Someone told me to ask an Englishman
To write this down on paper for me. Is this word 'fiercely' correct?
It sounds funny.
I have been ejected from more restaurants
                      in yr country than in any other.
Our waiters are not like yours. They are very male. They are
                      not embarassed to embrace you,
Press their moustaches against yr ear & tell you to leave,
Whilst holding yr waist in a tight grip.
It feels very unusual, but Englishmen think it more direct & honest
And grow to like it. And if you can
Wrestle the bloomers off the swarthy women of my country
You've had it, my friend, you're done for. When a Bosnian woman
Presses you to eat, you may not rise from the table
Until you are dead with exhaustion. You must experience
What it means to go beyond gratification.
Then you will understand. Ah, we are too patriotic, I know,
And when we kiss
Often it is kinder to put a knife in someone's ribs. But we are very
        gentle people.
We have the biggest mosquitoes.
Strangely, the nights here are vacant of whine. How do you sleep?
I was caught in a storm
Driving my melons to market. The old horse skipped a little

48

And then fell into the Drina, turning it red. All
The opened faces of the melons began to talk in prophecies. They
    said:
Stand up & go to London. Ask an Englishman to write this down:
'My name's John Bosnia, I have lost my cart & my crop,
And before you throw me out of this restaurant
I am going to read you this poem.'

Not a Sirventes Exactly

Sitting on the beach at Le Lavandou
                    thinking of troubadours,
And how many kilometers driven
                    the last few days,
Berlin to Mainz, down thru Chablis,
The high song of Provençal
                    whitening the road.
And I think of the Chateau,
And the two gold prospectors,
                    both drunk,
We talked with till late, proprietress
                    bringing the *Framboise*,
And of Bertrand de Born & Arnaut Daniel,
                    melody of a language
Civilised by poetry & war,
Gold in the rivers of France, unexpectedly,
And the question Gilles proposes:
Êtes-vous par tempérament artiste ou technicien?

Christian, getting drunker, had you on yr feet
                    serving the men coffee.
(You with yr modern independence
                    made suddenly obedient,
Yr worth
        the envy of others.)
And the pretty daughter of the proprietress
                    turned on him:
'You macho!'
        (Sos pretz a las autras enoia)

Next morning we took our leave
                    meeting no one,
Dawn fragrant with alcohol.
I still held the feel of you,
                E sembla conil de l'esquina,
Like a young rabbit quivering
                    under my hand.

And here we are, pale
(White as hawthorn blossom)
                in this Mediterranean ghetto,
Blancha pel cors com flors d'espina,
Aggressive, waitressy little bums
                        on strut patrol,
Red thighs & wordy T-shirts of customers,
No song in my pocket, grumpy
The way troubadours can be,
Fretful in love
                and in accommodation,
With a phone card instead of a horse,
A fast food joint instead of a kitchen...

The indignation
The dissatisfaction

The song...

Love Poem for the Loved One

She's sure to come.
Despite yourself you set off to meet her,
Walk for hours along a track
Used only by itinerant beekeepers.
In space suits, they bend over the swarm's levity,
Looking for the loved one, drawing
Out the files of honeycomb, their faces
Like honey itself, raising
A gloved hand to you, as you go on.

It seems impossible anyone shd walk this mountain edge.
Narrowness of the way makes passing
A hands-on-waist dance without words.
When you have passed her, distance enlarges to the power of two,
But she must take a job, in the inn naturally,
Serving at tables you may eventually see from afar.

It is springtime, & the lake is adjacent.
She dances for the men who are waiting for the ferry,
Prisoners from the jail, throwing themselves upon the grass.
She dances for the customers, then for the prisoners,
You can hear the washing up being done in the hotel.
Take out paper & pen, record what has entered yr mind.
For the prisoners, she takes off her blouse:
Freedom, freedom, freedom.

You write the word over & over again in the notebook,
Watching those gaolbirds, who regard you curiously.
Why are you watching them, & not this dance?
This dance that whirls & makes white spray from the air?
They have certainly committed unmentionable atrocities.
This dance whose beauty is so painful to appraise?
To whom it is almost strange to lift yr eyes?

Love Poem for the Room

I have to invent the things we do,
It's too big, you tell me. I love it.
You always look thoughtful & ready to let go at the same time,
I like to be able to see the clock & watch the hands move.
We try to turn our faces away, as the curtain ripens with light.
You grow from that tiny circlet like a dream.

Then there's the moment when you hesitate.
I wonder what wd happen if you called my bluff?
The only thing I have that I can give is what I get,
I'm a missionary, addicted to the way you say yes.

So to the moment when you skid off yr smile:
I see that slight self-consciousness transformed.
It's become something quite deliberate & unplanned,
As you trample over me on all fours.

Love Poem for the Postcard

If you can imagine the picture on the other side
This is for you:
A swing bridge near Dunquerque,
Rain & darkness, easy to miss on the swerve.
If you do not know the café
                    where the *Pelican Piss* goes down in draughts,
Blue overalled workmen smoke *tabac noir*,
I sense by yr fantastic lips
You'll know how to get to it,
That you have to cross that narrow place,
Deep, black water beneath
                    & that this is me
Approaching it too fast.

Love Poem for the Indolent

I was always too tired or too bored to remove yr panties,
Yr thighs looked so beautiful
Capped with that skimpy helmet of white cloth.
Shortly before the tennis-players began
Hitting each over the head with their racquets,
I closed the window to drown the hum of the grass,
Other sounds of nature also:
Leaf-mould arias, hedgehog duets, worm cantatas.
I closed my eyes & dreamed you were not here
But somewhere so magnificent & sumptuous
I cd not resist the temptation
To eat you alive.

In restaurants I fell into a stupefied revery,
Prior to terminating my interesting anecdotes.
Finishing them wd have endeared me to you considerably –
You wd have released yr bra straps in the car
And pushed yr nipples into my mouth,
But somewhere between the *Tagliatelle Verde* & the Mystery Play
The membrane of communication was forlornly snapped.

You grew tired of my interludes,
Yawningly removed yr clothes.
We fell into a discussion about India
Where neither of us had ever been.
You told me an Australian had made
                    unexpected love to you
One quiet Saturday afternoon,
Like a koala bear falling out of a tree into one's taxi.
I traced the whiteline of bra straps on yr golden flesh,
Cleared my throat & particularised
On the divagations of relationship,
The tributaries & streams of departure,
That make men & women
So wavelike, tidelike, stormlike, becalmed...

I couldn't desist from yr charms forever.
I began to think I shd love you
On the floor of every room in the house,
In the back of the car, stranded up to our hub caps in mud,
In a forest hiding place, so secret
It wd prove impossible to get out –
Lastly & unforgettably in the abandoned railway carriage
That started a mysterious journey by night
Across Holland.

Shake Up in Araby

They let you have a magic whistle
When blown, it brings them back, wherever they are
You get three blasts & three denials
An instantaneously concluded state of return

Of course they don't admit having left you
They're having a good time in the desert
Imagine it: a camp of camelskin tents
Clear bright water with a hawk reflected there

They move in their see-thru robes from canopy to canopy
During the cool, morning hours, carrying dates & coffee
On small, intricately-beaten copper trays
Visiting no one. Not even the prince. Keeping busy

They squat before wind-flensed sheep skulls
Their beautiful naked bottoms flash in the sun

A Sirventes Against Everybody

After Bertran de Born:

Be.m platz lo gais temps de pascor

I like the pleasant time of Easter:
Leaves & flowers bloom.
I like the bawdy of birds,
Thrilling woods with song.
I like it when, across fields
I see tents & pavilions rising,
And I am greatly soothed
To observe on the plain,
Horsemen, armed to the teeth.

O I like it when outriders
Put men & cattle to flight,
And a mailed throng gathers.
It delights my heart to see
Mighty castles under serious attack,
Ramparts & walls breached,
Men surrounded, at moat's brink,
Behind the staked palisades,
Desperately defending.

Our chief makes me jubilant,
Up front, leading the assault,
Mounted, iron-clad & fearless.
See how he nerves his men
To close-quarter recklessness
In his high-born service:
Everyone is eager to follow,
For no one can look at fame
Without a crack in the skull!

Shield & helmet riven apart –
I relish the heave & the smash.
Ah, to watch the affray start,
To see the opposition cut down,
Riderless horses of dead men
Running amok thru the mayhem!

Let every noble mother's son
Strike before the blood goes cold –
It's better to be dead than sorry!

Eating, drinking, sleeping...
They're nothing to shouts of
'Get 'em!' from all sides,
Horses whickering from ambush,
Followed by: 'Rescue! Save us!'
And I see rags of pennant
Fluttering on lance-hafts,
Where the fallen lie spitted,
The humble strewn with the great.

    Barons, mortgage what you have!
Yr castles, yr cities, yr towns,
Sooner than not go to war!

    And listen, fool,
Tell that hesitating boss of yrs
Too much PEACE is bad for you!

The Awful Ignominy of My Father's Death

We put him on the bed & he groaned.
We called the doctor on our tin-can telephone.
The doctor seemed to be counting haystacks in his mind.
Then the ambulance came,
A Gryphon & a Hoarse Hat Wearer.
They had a stretcher like a corridor.
My mother said: 'All the time I've known him
He's never done anything like that before.'
How long had she known him, after all?
Not a man for the ladies really,
More a man for the well-chosen word.
They took away his education, left only
Priceless, urine-steeped volumes
Under the bed.

That was that really.
In the hospital at Steglitz
He had a half-jointed grin,
The other half had fallen down a hole in his trouser leg.
A lady folded him into all kinds of shapes.
He slopped backwards & forwards like a highly intelligent pancake,
He was a thumb that had lost the route to its mouth.
She was obviously highly-trained.
Where did you get this training, I wanted to say:
The Florida Everglades?
Flamingoes write hate letters to Walt Disney, you know!
The expertise of her doing good was
A warning light on the jetliner before it crashes.
I mumbled:
Put him back in the drink & call the Royal Air Force!

Just before my Dad had his crow-like discomfiture with the branch
        he was sitting on,
He & I had had a bit of an argument about the nature of the tree,
Whether it was a Birch or an Oak or an alabaster mock-up of a Baobab.
Now his mouth was propped open with a darning mushroom,
The part of him that hadn't been poleaxed by a mad aardvark
Was saying: 'Just let me out of this flesh-prison
And I'll put these people straight on matters pertaining to everything!'

It was disgusting. I was the monotonous person
Who wd soon drive home by myself.
He wd fly back horizontally to the place he had last been vertical in.

I only saw him once more alive. They were teaching him to read.
Gigantic seagulls were walking all over the grey beach of his belly,
Laying eggs in the hairy cleft of his thighs.
'I've already done this,' he said, closing the book.
The nurses had kid-glove eyes.
They were the kind that wd have asked Julius Caesar if he was
          feeling better now.
I thought suddenly we'd gone on an excursion,
As if one of those old steam trains had puffed into a wood,
And the carriage door opened & everybody got out,
And it was summer,
So we said 'What a wonderful place for a party!'
Opened our hampers & popped the champagne corks,
Raised our glasses and sang 'Never trust a man who doesn't drink!'
Meanwhile my father struggled to voice a reprimand:
'Never trust a man who does!'
Which we couldn't hear, him being inaudible & so on.
And then we threw the empty glasses into the trees,
And I said 'Cheerio!' I'd see him in a month or so,
We'd talk then, even tho I knew
The railway was due for closure, no way of getting back,
And soon they'd build a supermarket
Just where his bed
Grew shady in the leaves.

The last time I saw my father
He had shrunk to the size of a matchbox.
He was very neat & pale.
He was singing *The Teddy Bear's Picnic* under his breath.
The undertaker was a very practical man:
He carried a spade, some rosewater, a pack of playing cards (all aces)
          & a car battery.
He kept saying things like:

All You Have To Do
Is Decide
What Not To Write On The Stone

Then he put the jump leads on my father's toes.

Time & Western Man

She saws at the bars of my cage
She frowns. She pauses
She goes to the sink
She makes herself a cup of tea
She has a hammer & cold chisel
She comes back looking refreshed. Her gown
Slips from her shoulders & she is lovely
So tall & naked I have to turn away
I stare thru a window. She takes
No notice of me & I yearn to hold her
When my back is turned, she's invisible
She fixes minute particles of explosive to my cage
There is a tremor. I feel everything shake
Close up, inspecting the damage, I can see
The smooth stain of her face, the clearness of her eyes
The firm tenderness of her breasts
Never once do we look at each other directly
She goes away into a corner
She fidgets

She's thinking

An Exciting Life

I

I saw the sunshine
become a hospital

in whose corridors
I gathered mote beams

like crosses
into my heart

I was a ghost, naturally
they went right thru me

I tried to step over them
under them

but thru every window
of the hospital, & it was all window,

came the surgical
shafts of brightness

& lit the empty dust whirl
of the person

I look thru
& am

II

I was in a garden
of the kind asylum

everything flowered
calm, slobbering lunatics

silent old women
locked in their spines

gesturing psychopaths
jumping up & down on their desires

I walked thru their presences
feigning a dignified absence

until I came to the girl
beyond the wire fence

To be precise
she was 14 years old

looking in at me
with her fingers gripping the wire

How old was I?
What kind of person was I?

Was I middle-aged?
Was I big or small? *'How's*

yr ego?' the dwarf said
playing bouncy with a ball.

He was agile as a squirrel,
rolling his eyes at the girl

in the dusk, the mad
electromagnetic dusk...

He hopped into the driving seat
of his big black pantechnicon

'Let's go,' he said
'They're waiting for collection!'

III

Oh well, we
went down the middle

then we went down the side
Chaffinches beeped from bridges

There were tears in our eyes
from wondering

Then we saw the sea
Our hair streamed

Everyone was very quiet
so as not to disturb the fish

I saw a gleaming cross in the clouds
& the head of the devil behind

& a fine golden dust
between the parting of yr thighs

'Time for solitude!' cried the dwarf
putting an end to our beginning

I felt two ghostly shapes
help me from the cab

thru the moaning gateway
down into The Vaults

It was cool & dark in there,
It was welcoming, welcoming...

There was just one single step,
the one we had left to make

'Now!' cried the dwarf
In the direction of each other

NOTES TO THE POEMS

Looking Over The Wall
The Berlin Wall was 155 kilometres of concrete round the western half of the city, turning Westberlin into an island. The West used it as a sort of blackboard. A piece of graffiti which rather summed up this function was: *'They came, they saw, they did a little shopping.'* In 1988 Erich Honecker, making one of the few official GDR references to it, said: 'This wall will be standing in fifty, even a hundred years time.'

Ausländer
Usually translated as *foreigner, immigrant* & *alien* are other meanings which are included within its scope of reference.

Das Doppelgehen
The noun *Doppelgänger* means (literally) a double.

On the Island
Westberlin: East German lower-case demotion of West Berlin.
Eck-kneipe: Corner pub.
Brücke der Einheit: Unity Bridge, otherwise known as *Glienicker Brücke.* It spans the Wannsee, linking Potsdam with Berlin.
Treffendes Angebot: An offer that hits the spot.
Wirtschaftswunder: The West German 'economic miracle'.
Das gläserne Pferd ist unbezahlbar, einfach nicht zu bezahlen: The glass horse is priceless, simply unaffordable.

The Turning Point
Ficken Tut Gut: Fucking does you good. *Hauswart:* Caretaker.
Rote Rathaus: The seat of Berlin city government, on Alexanderplatz. Red brick.

The Kiss
Zimmerpflanzen: Indoor plants.

Not a Sirventes, Exactly
Sirventes: A verse-polemic or diatribe.
Framboise: Alcoholic raspberry juice.
Êtes-vous par tempérament artiste ou technicien? Do you have an artistic or a scientific temperament?
The phrases of Provençal are translated in the text.

A Sirventes Against Everybody
Before somebody writes to tell me that *baudor* is not bawdy, & *ombratge* is not ambush, I wd like to say that this is a version, not a literal translation.